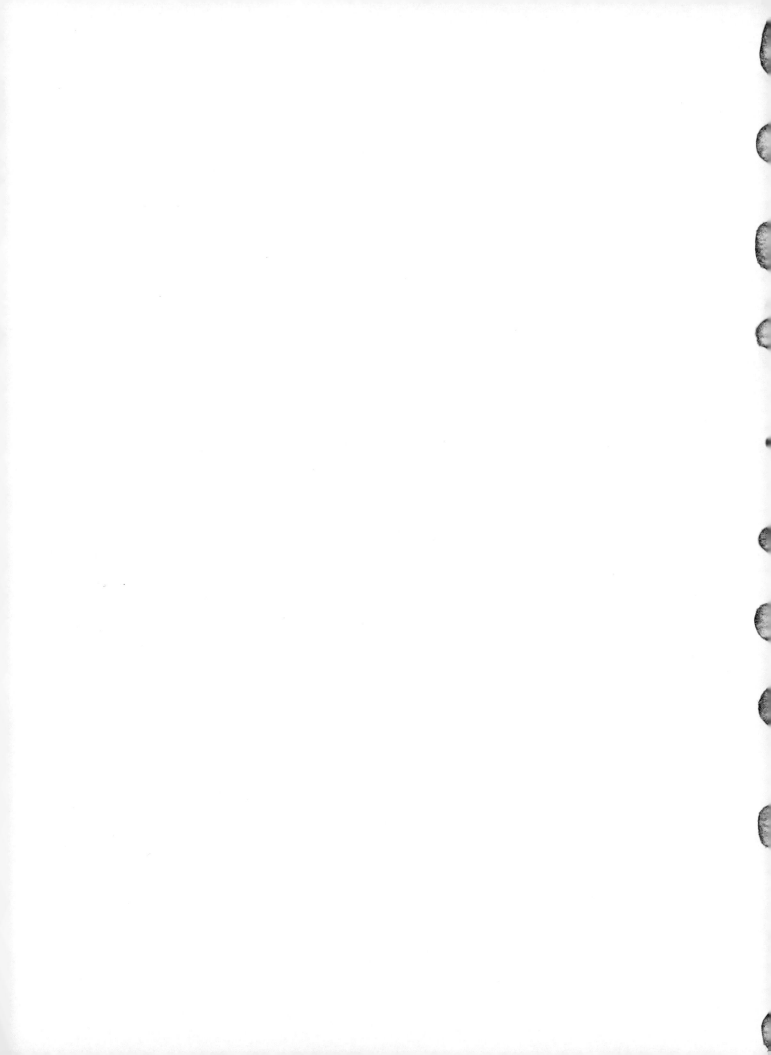

A *GARDEN* OF *VERSES* AND *INSPIRATIONAL* POEMS

GLORIA NIEDERMAN

AuthorHouse™
1663 Liberty Drive
Bloomington, IN 47403
www.authorhouse.com
Phone: 1 (833) 262-8899

Because of the dynamic nature of the Internet, any web addresses or links contained in this book may have changed
since publication and may no longer be valid. The views expressed in this work are solely those of the author and do
not necessarily reflect the views of the publisher, and the publisher hereby disclaims any responsibility for them.

Any people depicted in stock imagery provided by Getty Images are models,
and such images are being used for illustrative purposes only.
Certain stock imagery © Getty Images.

This book is printed on acid-free paper.

ISBN: 978-1-7283-7290-7 (sc)
ISBN: 978-1-7283-7291-4 (e)

Library of Congress Control Number: 2020916872

Print information available on the last page.

Published by AuthorHouse 10/30/2020

authorHOUSE®

A GARDEN OF VERSES AND INSPIRATIONAL POEMS

By Gloria Niederman

DEDICATION

In memory of my mother- Doris P. Maida whose goodness and generosity were endless.

When Mom entered into the everlasting light, my souls' candle blew out. But I realized loves' flame still burned in my heart. Death could not keep us apart.

ROSES

ALL KINDS OF ROSES CAN ENCHANT, A GARDEN ON A SUMMER MORN.
WITH STUNNING COLORS THEY'RE FRAGRANT. CLIMBING TRELLISES
THEY ADORN, SMALL BORDER BLOSSOMS THAT ARE SCANT.
IN LATE SUMMER ROSES LAZILY LOLL, LIKE A LITTLE GIRLS' TIRED CHINA DOLL.

THE ROSEBUDS' PERFUME SCENT BRINGS PLEASURE AND DRIED LEAVES ARE A TIMELESS
TREASURE.

THESE ROSES HAVE A SATINY GLOSS- LOVELY BOUQUETS FOR A BRIDE TO TOSS.

Apricot nectars' scent is alluring. With leathery leaves it is enduring.

The Blue Moon rose is beguiling, some lavender buds are smiling.

It starts sparkling at daybreak like stars that try to stay awake.

Lavender rose - Roses by color - Wikimedia Commons

On a pillow of white surrounded
Color Magic seems ready to doze

CINDERELLA IS PINK AND TINGED WITH WHITE. SHE STARTS SEARCHING FOR HER LOST SLIPPER. OUTSIDE, A PUMPKIN IS WAITING FOR HER. MAGIC CAROUSEL IS LOSING ITS SPELL. SHE COULD NOT RETURN BEFORE MIDNIGHT.

FAST GROWING ENCHANTRESS IS BURNING BRIGHT. THEIR FULL CUPS OPEN LIKE HALOS OF LIGHT.

Compassion rose is soft-hearted; grieving for the departed.

Her sympathy has no end. For each flower she's a friend.

Yellow cottage rose is elaborate. In the evening their highlights scintillate.

PINK IVORY ROSE PETALS ARE POINTED.

THEIR LAYERED BLOOMS OPEN SOFT-SCENTED.

THE LARGE ROSE-RUFFLED HYBRID TEA BLOOM, THROUGH SUMMER AND AUTUMN WITH SWEET PERFUME.

This gorgeous rose has a secret to keep. She only whispers it when she's asleep. Her heart-shaped center beats quietly, almost revealing the mystery.

The fragrant scotch rose has plenty of thorns. But in spring and summer they're not forlorn.

SHEER PINK ICE BLENDS SOME LIGHT AND SHADOW-
IN A MYRIAD OF COLOR GLOW, WITH SATIN-SHEENED BUDS
LIKE RIBBON AND STREAKS OF LIGHTBEAMS FROM HEAVEN.

AMBER CREAM ROSE IS A LARGE-FLOWERED BELLE, OPENING LIKE A BIRD FROM ITS
SHELL.

The pointed blooms of this royal queen, has a pretty hue and is pristine. She has been seen leaving her throne. She didn't want to be alone.

The lovely pink gems love the twilight. They go on glowing throughout the night.

PERENNIALS

Bleeding heart grows best in shade; but by late summer they fade.

Pure candytuft is demure. At night, with tulips they're not obscure.

Bright yellow daisies, watching azure skies; with their cushioned center they mesmerize.

Before snow begins to melt, hellebores flowers are felt.

From March to May a lent rose, in shady woods start to pose.

Iris petals are wavy and bent; with prisms of color radiant.

Delphiniums blossoms are swaying. Like a kaleidoscope is turning.

Pastel colors are an artists' dream. Pink, lilac and white catch a sunbeam.

Poppies come in colors of a rainbow. In fields these hardy ones brilliantly grow. They're swaying in the wind with splendor. Its opened cups are a wonder.

Scabiosa petals are pink and blue.. In summer they give a breathtaking view.

Annuals

Begonias can be started inside, but these colorful bulbs cannot hide. This soft-layered red, pink or white bloom; cascading from pots, cheer up a room. Transplant in the shade when frost is past and these wonderful flowers will last.

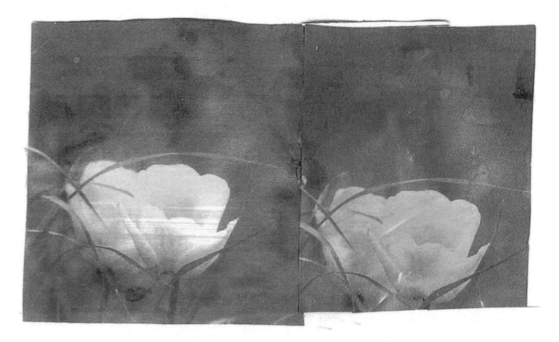

These pretty flax are sapphire blue. Although they are tough and do not need rain, they still love to catch the morning dew. Their delicate looks may tell a lie, since the sturdy flowers won't say good-bye.

Calla lilies are smooth as pearl, with petals soft as velour.

Gerberas, roses and Queen Anne's lace, have beauty, dignity and grace.

Radiating from centers of spun gold, ivory white spikes of cosmos unfold.

Dahlia seeds like soil that's warm. Soon beautiful flowers will form. Remember to keep roots cool. They'll flash in light like a jewel.

Lilac clusters, lavender and white, shine from chandeliers and candlelight.

Lisianthus are smooth as lace, dazzling in a porcelain vase.

Peonies in most colors are found. In autumn they will fall to the ground. It is best to plant them alone; but in borders, use stepping stones. If it's privacy that you want, large blossoms hide windows in front.

BIENNIALS

BACHELOR BUTTONS ARE SINGLE, BUT WITH CHAMOMILE THEY MINGLE.

THE BELLFLOWER HAS ICE-BLUE POISE-ONE OF SUMMER'S COLORFUL JOYS.

English daisies bloom from May to August. Rose, lavender and white plants are robust.

Foxglove have thimble-like flowers, on stalks a butterfly settles. A captivating work of art; called digitalis for the heart.

Tall hollyhocks bloom with glamour and grace. Ravishing beauty fills a garden space.

Pansies have iridescent fronts. In late summer grow for four months.

ICYCLES HANG: FROM ABOVE. THAW MY ICY HEART WITH LOVE. GIVE WATER TO THE PLANT BELOW. SEE THE BEAUTIFUL FLOWER GROW.

The lovely crocuses rise, reaching mountain sunset skies.

BULBS

Crocus is springs' early sign. Daffodils grow in a line.. Rain falls in a cupped daffodil, opening creamy in April.

Tulips and lilacs in a field kiss; with forget-me-nots-a gardeners bliss.

Gladiolas come in many sizes. Multi-colors bring summer surprises.

White, drift fragrance in the air at night. Roots are very tuberous and blooms are luxurious.

Fragile hyacinths are exquisite. On luminous nights that are star-lit.

Ranunculas appear in late june, with ball-shaped flowers like a full moon.

THE SWEET PEA VINE IS IN NEED OF RAIN. ITS RUFFLED PINK FLOWER CAN'T REMAIN. THE TWINING VINE, CLIMBING A ROCK WELL, SLOWLY INTO THE WATER FELL.

The whistling wind sings a lovely note; through breezes on tulips silky spring coats.

Snowdrops gather in a crowd praying as their heads are bowed.

Gardenia are fragrant, waxy and white. Swirls of petals are a pretty sight.

Tall hibiscus, with red or pink lace; for childrens' games is a hiding place.

Hills of hydrangeas love a sunny day. Blooms can be dried for a winter bouquet.

THIS ORCHID GLIMMERS ON SUNNY DAYS. THE LAVENDER SHIMMERS IN ITS RAYS.

A SWEET WINDFLOWER INSPIRES, A NIGHTINGALE TO FLY HIGHER.

SUNROSE HALIMUM'S CENTER IS PEARL WHITE. TO BLOSSOM, GOLD BUDS NEED DRY SUNLIGHT. EACH FLOWER OPENS FOR ONLY A DAY. ON A HILLSIDE IS A DARLING DISPLAY.

ADORNING ALTARS IS SOFT ORCHIDS' FELT. WE STARED AT THE AWESOME WONDER AND KNELT. THE RARE GOLDEN-WHITE CROWN IS EXOTIC. INSPIRING THE PRAYERS OF A MYSTIC.

WILDFLOWERS

DANDELIONS ON AN OPEN FIELD LAY, UNTIL STRONG WINDS BLOW WISHES AWAY.

THIS RARE IRIS' INTRIGUING DESIGN, HAS STUNNING PURPLE COLOR LIKE WINE. BEAUTIFUL RUFFLES ARE GREETING THE DAY. YELLOW SUNSHINE ON THE PETALS LAY. THE DARK SHADOWS IN IT REMIND ME, OF JESUS' JOURNEY TO CALVARY. THE OUTSTRETCHED BULBS-THE SHAPE OF A CROSS; INCANDESCENT WITH A SATIN GLOSS.

These flowers have a silky sheen. In gardens everywhere are seen. On a veranda hanging high, catching a weary butterfly. Shades of white, violet pink or reds, have luscious ruffles in baskets or beds.

White Concrete House · Free Stock Photo

4/28/2020

✕

Roses and four-o-clocks on a lawn, illuminated with sunshine at dawn. Marigolds and delphiniums, tall and short, surround your home like a beautiful fort.

Snow-like trees are cottonwood. Bending in the wind they stood. To the violet mountains they bow.. Sunrise on the horizon now.

Buried shells are scattered on the beach; the receding tide is out of reach. Water-filled conches and clams will pray; the hurts of broken shells wash away.

AS THE SUN IS SETTING IN THE WEST, SILHOUETTES OF NEWBORN CLOUDS PROTEST.
A CUP AND SAUCER-LIKE ORB STILL SHINES, RESTING ON FLAMING HORIZON LINES.

Pushing up from the dark womb of the earth, is sunrise like an infant at birth.

A MOTHER RABBIT SEES HER BABY HARE, FLOATING ON A CLOUD IN THE AIR. 'A TROLL
IS TAKING MY BABY AWAY! TO A GUARDIAN ANGEL SHE WILL PRAY.

FROM "WHAT A WONDERFUL WORLD" BY ANNE MURRAY AT ANNMURRAY.COM

Rock formations hold back the tide, where thousands of sea creatures hide.

CHRISTMAS TREE DRESSED IN PSARKLING WHITE ON A CLOUD OF COTTONY SNOW. SHINE FOR ALL THE LONELY TONIGHT. NRIGHTEN ONE LIFE WHOSE HOPE IS GONE. TELL A SAVIOUS'S BIRTH AT DAWN.

Shadows on mountain peaks rise and fall, like children playing on a see-saw.

WHILE ANGELS LAY ON A PILLOWED CLOUD; LIGHTNING, THEN THUNDER WILL CLAP OUT LOUD.

SNOWFLAKES ARE LIKE STARS FALLING FROM SPACE.

EACH UNIQUE- PATTERNED IN CRYSTAL LACE.

A POLAR BEAR LOOKED SURPRISED TO BE, STANDING ON AN ICEBERG IN THE SEA. HE IS AFRAID HE WILL SLIP AND FALL. HE NEEDS TO MAKE AN SOS CALL.

AS I LOOKED DOWN FROM MY JET'S FLIGHT, I SAW AN UNUSUAL SIGHT. HOW COULD A HUGE ICEBERG BE IN THE MIDDLE OF THE SEA. I LOVED ITS STRUCTURE OF WHITE AND BLUE AND THE OPENING GAVE ME A VIEW OF FLOATING CLOUDS LIKE A NET ON THE ENDLESS OCEAN MET. BUT WITH A GUST AND SUDDEN THAW, MY MIRACLE MIRAGE DID FALL. THEN WRITTEN ON THE SKY ABOVE WAS FAITH, HOPE AND A PEACEFUL DOVE.

SNOWCAPPED TREES ARE REACHING HIGH, AGAINST THE MOON'S WINTER SKY. BENT TOGETHER WHISPERING STORIES, LIKE TIMELESS PHOTOGRAPH MEMORIES.

From Velvet blue the cold is felt. The icy birds and creatures won't melt. His fingered rays like a candle glow. In a wonderland of drifted snow.

WINTER SCENES

ON A PINE TREE SO SVELT, TINY CREATURES START TO MELT. A FLUFFY LAMB AND SNOWMEN DRIP, WHILE OTHER WHITECAPS KEEP THEIR GRIP. IN THE MOUNTAINS' CANYON DEEP, GHOSTLY SOUNDING ECHOS WEEP. REVERBERATING ON THE WALL, FADING INTO A MUFFLED CALL.

Pebbles' shadows and flowers shoot, on the ground with bitterroot. Dry grass and rosy buds pray, hoping for a rainy day.

Pebbles' shadows and flowers shoot, on the ground with bitterroot. Dry grass and rosy buds pray, hoping for a rainy day.

ALL THE DAISIES SEEM TO FUSS. WILDFLOWERS ARE CHOKING US. THEIR YELLOW EYES STARTED TO CRY; WAITING FOR THE RAIN TO DRY.

HILLS AND PINE TREES EMBRACE THE DEW, ACROSS A PANORAMIC VIEW. SWIRLS OF CLOUDS WITH THE FOG REACH ACROSS THE VIOLET MOUNTAINS AND PEAT MOSS.

YELLOWSTONE FALLS POUR INTO A BOG. ALONG GRANITE AND MISTY FOG. SLOPING HILLS AND EVERGREEN, GOING INTO A RAVINE.

Fingering branches reach the autumn pines. In one of natures' loveliest designs. The wrinkled beagle-like stones, rests on the skies inky tones.

ON ANCIENT RUINS OF A CAVE, THE SHADOW OF THREE WISE MEN WAVE. THEIR GIFTS TO THE BABY THEY TAKE, REFLECTED ON THE GLASSY LAKE.

Mysteries painted by his hand-rock shadows and sunlight fade. He's reaching down to the water, 'be not afraid'. He'll always be our guide, to save us in high tide.

Ebony streaks holding back the sun,
A mysterious angel from heaven
Watching the shrouded figure above
Is natures' contrast of hate and love.

Roses are climbing a trellis wall. Hanging branches will gracefully fall.
An ivory angel in the spring, make clematis and bluebells ring.

A LOST SOUL SAVE BY JESUS HAND. FROM THE SINKING OF HOT QUICKSAND.

WHEN WE PRAY, FROM ROSES FALL SOME DEW DROPS. FROM PURGATORY THE LOST SOUL FLAME STOPS.

SOULS ARE FORGOTTEN EVERY DAY, UNTIL SOMEONE REMEMBERS TO PRAY. LILY-OF-THE-VALLEY BELLS, THE MERCY OF GOD IT TELLS.

GEMS FOR SOULS

IN JANUARYS' DEEP FREEZE, SAY ON GARNET ROSARIES, KEEP IN MIND SOULS WHO ARE SORRY WAITING TO LEAVE PURGATORY.

ON FEBRUARY, AMETHYST BEADS, SAY PRAYERS FOR THOSE WHO ARE IN MUCH NEED. OUR LOVED ONES WE REMEMBER. FIRE IS QUENCHED TO EMBER.

MARCH'S STONE-LIKE THE SEA OF BLUE-GREEN, IS THE ROSARY'S GEM AQUAMARINE. HELP THE SOULS TO BE RESCUED FROM FLAME. FOR US THEY WILL ONE DAY DO THE SAME.

APRIL-LIGHT FROM THE LUMINOUS DIAMOND GLOW ON EACH MYSTERY LET OUR MERCY GROW. FOR DYING SOULS WE CAN SAY, A ROSARY EVERYDAY

MAYS' EMERALD IN A WATER-FILLED JAR; SAYING PRAYERS FOR SOULS THAT HAVE SUNK SO FAR. AWARE OF THEIR PLEAS FOR AID, A NOVENA CAN BE MADE. AS THE EMERALD FLOATS ON TOP, THE BURNING TORMENT WILL STOP.

JUNES' PRAYERS FOR THOSE WHO FELL AND DROWNED IN A DEEP WELL. WE'RE HEARING THEIR WAILS OF THIRST. THEY WILL NO LONGER BE CURSED. RAIN WATER AND THE WIND TELLS, NEW PEARLS TO COME FROM THEIR SHELLS.

ON JULYS' RUBY ROSARY, REMEMBER JESUS'S AGONY. LONG AGO HE ROSE FROM THE DEAD. LET HEAVEN'S BEAMING RAYS BE STAIRS, TO LEAD SOULS FROM OUR FERVENT PRAYERS. TO ETERNITY THEY'LL BE LEAD.

AUGUST-OLIVE GREEN PERIDOT; LIFT A SOUL THAT IS BURNING HOT. SEE THEM TRYING TO REPENT. SOON TO HEAVEN THEY ALL WENT.

SEPTEMBER-PRAYING ON SAPPHIRE BEADS SO BLUE, WE HOPE IT CAN SAVE MORE THAN A FEW. FROM THEIR SOULS' TERRIBLE ABYSS, WE'LL BRING THEM TO HEAVENLY BLISS.

OCTOBER'S ONYX ROSARY BEAD, WE PRAY SOULS WILL NO MORE BE IN NEED. WE HOPE THAT JESUS THEY WILL SEE, AND BRING THEM TO ETERNITY.

NOVEMBER'S TOPAZ ROSARIES-A DECADE FOR TEN SOULS ARE PLEAS. FROM THE DEAD NONE REMAIN. TO HEAVEN'S GATE THEY CAME.

DECEMBER-CHRISTMAS TURQUOISE ROSARY SHINE; FROM OUR PRAYERS BRING LOVE DIVINE. THAT FROM THE FIERY HEARTH, SOULS WILL RISE IN THEIR REBIRTH.

A WINTER JOURNEY

IN NAZARETH LONG AGO, AMID THE WINTER SNOW, TWO WEARY TRAVELERS SAY, 'THERE IS NO PLACE WE CAN STAY'. MARY WAS TIRED FROM THE RIDE, BUT SHE HAD JOSEPH BY HER SIDE. THEN A STABLE WAS FOUND, UPON THE FROZEN GROUND. A NIGHT OF PAIN WAS GONE, AND AT THE BREAK OF DAWN, UPON A CRADLE FILLED WITH HAY, JESUS WAS BORN ON CHRISTMAS DAY.

WINTER-2007

THE WINTER HAD SOME BALMY DAYS, BUT WINTER IS NOT FAR AWAY. MY ACHES TELL ME TIME MARCHES ON..

THE DAYS OF MY YOUTH ARE LONG GONE. A LONE BIRD IS CRYING AND TREES ARE STILL SIGHING, 'WHEN WILL YOU SEND THE SNOWMAN AWAY?

SOON ICE IS GONE, AS SPRING WILL DAWN.

WINTER-2014

JANUARY 21ST-IN THE SNOW WE ARE IMMERSED. COTTON CANDY FROM THE SKY, FALLING MANY INCHES HIGH. BLOWING, DRIFTING, FLYING BY. IN THE MIDDLE OF THE NIGHT, BLANKETS EVERYTHING IN WHITE. TEMPERATURES ARE DIPPING LOW. NOW LANDSCAPES GIVE A GLOW. AS THE SUN STARTS SHINING BRIGHT, WINTER IS A PRETTY SIGHT. MOUNDS OF NEW SNOW FORMING CLUMPS, COVERING BUSHES WITH LUMPS-CAMELS, IN DESERTS OF WHITE. IT'S A LOVELY BUT EERIE SIGHT. A TREASURY OF PHOTOGRAPHS TO TAKE. AS MEMORIES FROZEN IN TIME WE MAKE.

SPRING SCENES

CLOUDS WITH THUNDERS' RESONANCE; RAINDROPS ON THE SIDEWALK DANCE. AFTER NIGHTS' DARK SHROUD, LIGHT BEAMS THROUGH THE CLOUD. SPRINKLE DEW FOR ME AND FOR YOU.

SOFT AS FAIRY WING, A BABY BIRD CAN SING. IS IT A SIGN OF SPRING, OR A MOM'S ABANDONING?

A CROCUS HEAD STARTS TO POP UP, AND GREETED BY A BUTTERCUP; WITH COLORS OF YELLOW AND LAVENDER MAKE ROBINS IN A HOLLOW TREE STIR. A BLOOM OF

DAFFODIL CAN MAKE A WINTER BIRD THRILL. THE PUSSY WILLOW'S VELVET TOUCH, ON AN INFANTS' HAND, SOOTHES SO MUCH.

NIGHT TURNS TO DAY, LIGHT THROUGH THE CLOUDS PEEK. IT'S THEIR LITTLE GAME OF HIDE-AND-SEEK. IN A WHITE WEB, THE SPIDER SPINS, + ANOTHER SILK THREAD BEGINS. ON MILES AND MILES OF OPEN HILLS, A SHOWER OF DEWDROPS ON THE PLAIN SPILLS.

NATURE IN SUMMER

WISTERIA IN ALL COLORS CAN TWINE, ALONG CLEMATIS WHITE FLOWERING VINE. IN HONEYSUCKLE, THE BEES ARE ENTRANCED; IN WIND CARRIED FAR A SWEET FRAGRANCE. DON'T BE AFRAID OF THE QUEEN BEES' STINGER; SHE KNOWS SHE'LL DIE IF SHE STABS YOUR FINGER.

THE CATERPILLAR'S UGLY BUT BENIGN. AFTER A METAMORPHOSIS IT'S FINE. WITH PRETTY COLORS AND TEXTURED DESIGN, FROM A LARVAE TO CHRYSALIS COMES OUT A BEAUTIFUL INSECT TO FLY ABOUT.

Lightning bugs might warn, there's a thunderstorm. A haze field can form, but they could be gone in a flash. The thunder still comes in a crash. From clouds, shower a storm surge. When tidal waves and sky merge, like opera and symphony are splashing in agony.

Out of a secretive cloister, came a smooth pearl from an oyster. The rounded gem was milky white; on sand dunes, a childs' delight.

Along the cemetery stones, wildflowers protect the bones.

NATURE'S FRIENDS

THE DUSKY RED AND BLUE TURN TO GRAY. A GROAN FROM A TREE BRANCH SEEMS TO SAY, "DON'T WORRY, LITTLE SPARROW, MY FRIEND,; THE EARTHS' DARK SHADOW IS AT NIGHTS' END. IN THE BLINK OF MY EYE, DAYLIGHT RETURNS TO THE SKY.

AFTER WINTER, HE'S READY TO COME OUT. OF WHAT CREATURE AM I SPEAKING ABOUT. A SOFT WHISTLE'S HEARD AT DAWN AND DAYS END. WHAT DO YOU SAY, MY PERPETUAL FRIEND? 'I'M AWAKE ALL NIGHT BUT TOMORROW I'LL RISE, AND MOAN SOME MORE WITH THAT GLINT IN MY EYES. AND YOU, SHARP-NOSED FELLOW, STOP TORMENTING THAT WOOD. A RED COLORED FEATHER FELL ON MY WING." THE WIND GUST SAYS WITH A SIGH, "WELCOME SPRING, YOU SHOULD LEARN HOW TO SING. STARLING, COME OUT OF YOUR NEST, AND GREET THE DAY LIKE THE REST."

MR. OWL SAYS TO A WEEPING WILLOW TREE, "DON'T SHED A TEAR. I'M GONE FOR A TIME, BUT RETURN NEXT YEAR. WITH YOUR SWAYING BRING A SWEET FRAGRANCE NEAR".

A SQUIRRELS' RUNNING DOWN THE MAPLE TRUNKS' BARK; HEARS BLUEJAYS AND ROBINS SING IN THE DARK.

TREES REACHING HIGH AS A KITE. EERIE AS A STORMY NIGHT. BLOCKING SOME OF THE SUN'S LIGHT. SPRING BLOSSOMS THEY INVITE.

AUTUMN FALLS

AS THE SUN SINKS LOW AND STARTS TO FADE, THE ALMIGHTY HAND PULLS DOWN HIS SHADE. HALF OF THE EARTH MUST DARKEN TO NIGHT, WHILE THE OTHER WAKES TO MORNING LIGHT.

THE STAIN-GLASS WINDOWS CAST PRISMS OF LIGHT, WITH RAINBOW COLORS - A BEAUTIFUL SIGHT. ON WALLS, SHADOWS OF BRANCHES, THE WIND STIR. WONDERS OF CREATION WE REMEMBER.

THE CINNAMON SCENTS FILL THE AIR. OF CHANGING WEATHER BE AWARE.

THE COLORFUL LEAVES FROM THE WIND SWAY. NATURES' SWEEPER BLOWS THEM AWAY. GONE ARE THE YELLOW, RED, ORANGE TO BROWN. IT'S WINTER FIRST CALL. THEY'RE NOT HAPPY AT ALL.

CANDLE FLAMES SCENTED THE AIR ABOVE, LIKE THE HOLY SPIRIT SENDING LOVE. GLASS HOLDER FLICKERING, WAVING, AND DANCING. DRIPPING WAX IN THE CANDLEWICK SEEMS TO PLAY A MAGICIANS' TRICK.

NOSTALGIA

AS I HEARD THE GUSTY STORM WIND, MY OLD SQUEAKY FONT DOOR OPENED. DIFFERENT SCENTS FILLED THE LIVING ROOM. GARDENIA, ROSE AND ORCHID IN BLOOM. A TOUCH OF LAVENDER LILAC, OLD-FASHIONED MEMORIES BROUGHT BACK. AS I SAT ON THE VERANDA ENJOYING THE PINK AZALEA, THESES BEAUTIES OF NATURE BROUGHT MUCH DELIGHT; BEAUTIFUL FLOWERS FROM MORNING TO NIGHT.

January's scarlet sunset, is crimson as a bright garnet.

February's cold skies gray mist, turns to a purple amethyst.

March winds ruffle oceans green-blue, when the earth is waking anew.

April's sunshine like a diamond, glittering over a large pond.

May's opening buds are emerald, with blooming tulips pink and gold.

June's lovely roses with cream and white pearl, are sweet-scented as a baby girl.

On the cross, Jesus' precious blood shed. Burns in July's gem-ruby red.

August's heat shines in a brilliant jewel and is reflected in a large pool.

Through September's skies-blue as sapphire-into autumn's brisk air birds fly higher.

Through october's cool clouds an opal moon

Promises cold weather will be here soon.

November turns dark topaz with short days,

Ice crystal stars never cease to amaze.

December rain turns to a deep freeze.

Send us a snowstorm by christmas, please.

New snowfall has the sun's brilliant glare
at the dawn of morn when skies are fair
the last quarter moon with bent tips
has a dark veil of an eclipse. The foggy night
can't block the view and in morning leave sprinkled dew

into the earth, plant roots go deep
the skies open up and start to weep
while all the earth is sound asleep
seeds seek nourishment in the ground
like a soul whose thoughts are profound
until dawn turns the world around, skies change
from gray amethyst, to a shade of pink and gold
soft lights of sunrise unfold

The roses are withered and dwindling, as warm
autumn days are shortening
They're sad to be losing the sun's slants
with disappearing sweet fragrance.

in a storm summer roses almost drowned, until
continuous sunshine was found.
But some buds were getting too dry
Thirsty flowers wither and die.

THE SHINE OF ICE CRYSTALS ON THE LAKE, LIKE POLISHED SMOOTH ICING ON A CAKE. SKATERS GLIDE IN FIGURES OF EIGHT, WITH JUMPS AND TWIRLS ELBORATE.

WHERE MOONLIT ICE WAS GLASSY AND SLICK, THE SOUND OF SKATERS BREAKING ICE CLICK.

SAND EMPTIED INTO AN HOUR GLASS, SHOWING THAT OUR LIFE ON EARTH WILL PASS. AS THE LAST GRAIN OF SAND IS FOUND, GOD'S HAND IS TURNING IT AROUND.

THE YEARS OF OUR LIFE MAKE RIPPLES IN A LAKE. SEASONS THAT ARE CALM ON THE SURFACE GLOW, BUT THERE COULD BE A MURKY UNDERTOW.

THE DAYS OF LIFE ON EARTH FALL AND WITH IT COMES OUR CURTAIN CALL. DID WE PASS ON THE ROAD A POOR MANS' WAIL? WAS JESUS'S IMAGE ON OUR VEIL?

On Easter day, are the unturned stones?
Does our heart's tomb have old heavy bones?

Have little stones turned into rocks?
Can we still hear when the Saviour knocks?

The pastures gate has a broken lock.
The shepherd hunts for one of his flock.

O Lord, free us from our chains, of icy
and pouring rains; of the grief and
lonely days, until on your face we gaze.

Mountain lake images are a blur, as when
looking into a mirror. It's unclear and
out of focus. God's creation is mysterious.

REFLECTIONS ON HOLY EUCHARIST

THE HOST IS HELD WITHIN THE BEAUTIFUL MONSTRANCE. RADIATING FROM THE CENTER-EACH GOLD SPIKE IS LIKE A PERSON, A MEMBER OF YOUR BODY IN THE WORLD.

EVERYONE HAS THEIR OWN SPECIAL GIFT, SENDING YOUR LOVE OUT TO THOSE IN NEED. THE STEM OF THE VESSEL- THE CHURCH'S FOUNDATION LIKE JESUS HOLDING UP HIS PEOPLE.

OUR HEARTS CAN BE LIKE THE CIBORIUM, THE CENTER HOLDER WHERE JESUS IS CONTAINED. THE GOLD CIRCLING AROUND AS A CLOCK, WHERE OUR SPIRITUAL LIFE MAKES PROGRESS-MOVING FORWARD, NOT BACKWARD. THE CROSS AT THE TOP - IS THE MEANS TO OUR SALVATION, SUFFERING AS JESUS DID. HOLY EUCHARIST WAS INSTITUTED ON HOLY THURSDAY AT THE LAST SUPPER, AFTER OUR LORD FASTED IN THE DESERT FOR 40 DAYS.

BEHIND THE TABERNACLE OF GOLD
THE PRIEST CONSECRATED WINE AND BREAD
WITH HIS BODY AND BLOOD WE'RE FED

CHILDLIKE, PRESENT OURSELVES AT MASS
OUR SOULS WASHED LIKE STAINED WINDOWS GLASS
SO WE WILL SEE HIM MORE CLEAR
WHEN THE EUCHARIST IS NEAR

Open our hearts' tabernacle door, and give ourselves to those in need, and for us heavenly treasures store.

Eyes as clear as a sky of blue. For us Our Lady's love so true. Her blue gown is pristine.
After her life's 7 sorrows; in heaven she's our Queen.

Youth-the promise of velvet buds seems, like a pastel rainbow of dreams.

Middle age- comes in shades of blues. Youth is jaded in slate gray hues.
At dusk with sunset dreams will fade; new horizons of aging made.

Old age-Our eyes are losing sight; like dark violet black of night. Future uncertain as a mist. What's left to finish on my list.

The lovely lavender crocuses rises; reaching mountain sunset, painting the skies.

An umbrella is like a frown; until you turn it upside down. It's quickly filling up with rain; until sunshine is out again; and in the sky there is a rainbow, in orange, red, blue-green and yellow.

As I walked from my home on a hill, in the church the sun was shining still.
Sunbeams reach across the floor, to the tabernacle door.

Narcissus and bluebell, on Jacobs' ladder fell.
White handel roses that climb, in the morning look sublime.
Red and gold leaves twining in tapestry, autumn hibiscus droop in a curtsy.
Summer Fashions' creamy red buds flourished. Colors blend in a caress when nourished.

Feathery snow spreads in a cloak of gauze. Old-man winter throws crystals from his claws.
In the morning white sheep graze, as wildflowers eyes gaze at the royal blue skies.
All of nature will rise.
At the dawn there was a glistening sheen, on carpets of snow pristine.

The lambs quilted white wool, breathed in air crisp and cool. Groundhogs are hibernating, while some squirrels are still waiting.

After Jesus fell down the first time, with the cross He continued to climb.

Jesus meets Mary on the way; with the Disciples She will pray.

With Simon's help Jesus's cross was carried; but from the burden He wouldn't be freed.

After Jesus and Veronica met, on her veil, His face was covered with sweat.

As Jesus falls again, He is pushed by cruel men.

For Jesus the women cried sadly, but their children had His sympathy.

Jesus third fall would be His last, but His suffering wasn't past.

Jesus was stripped of His garment; as it was near the end of Lent.

Jesus on the cross was nailed; as Mary and the women wailed.

When Jesus closed His eyes in death, it took away His Mothers' breath.

1st Joyfu, sorrowful, luminous, and glorious mysteries

By the Holy Spirit, Mary conceives, but for Jesus's agony she grieves. On the water Jesus, John baptizes. After 3 days on Easter HE rises.

2nd Joyful, sorrowful, luminous, glorious mysteries

Jesus carried at the visitation, even through scourging His face wouldn't mar, from the water to wine transferred in a jar. After miracle cures, His ascension.

3rd Joyful, sorrowful, luminous, glorious mysteries

On Christmas in a stable He was born.
On Jesus's head put a crown of thorn.
Jesus's kingdom was proclaimed. On disciples heads
tongues of fire flamed.

4h Joyful, sorrowful, luminous, glorious mysteries

Jesus is taken to temple by Mary. Jesus, with the cross climbed to Calvary.
At the mount Jesus's transfigurational.
Taken by Jesus, is Mary's Assumption.

5th Joyful, sorrowful, luminous, glorious mysteries

Mary finds Jesus after three days.
On the cross, Jesus to His Father prays. The last supper's transubstantiation.
With Jesus is Mary's coronation.

From conception to the time of birth, we're shielded from the sorrows of earth. Safe from the dangers of the world; in our mothers' womb we are curled.

When daylight is scarce and dim, foil-wrapped fir trees endure in winter landscapes new and pure.

On the luminous earth, a spectrum glows; a palate of colors splashing rainbows.

Sunlight rays came after the rain. Sparkling teardrops of yellow and green.
Patterns continue again and again.
Lifes' mixture of intricate designs seen.

At daybreak the oceans' surface; colors bursting like shattered glass
At nightfall the moonlight's on display, along with stars coming out to pray.

The oceans may be far and wide, but our Saviour's the only guide.
The path is narrow and straight. To lead us to heavens'; gate.

Myriads of colors appear, on facets of a chandelier.
Danny, the dolphin swam in the tide.
I'm drowning, please help me, he cried.
A lovely fish heard the dolphin's wail.
Danny was saved by the mermaids' tail.

The passions of youth are not quite razed,
A spark still remains to set ablaze.
A story of life to old age,
I haven't yet turned the last page,
With fading eyesight nothing is clear,
There is beautiful music to hear.

The sound of a robin singing a note;
While shivering buds long for a coat.

Youth-the promise of velvet buds seems, like a pastel rainbow of dreams.

Middle age- comes in shades of blues. Youth is jaded in slate gray hues.
At dusk with sunset dreams will fade; new horizons of aging made.

Old age-Our eyes are losing sight; like dark violet black of night. Future uncertain as a mist. What's left to finish on my list.

Open our hearts' tabernacle door, and give ourselves to those in need, and for us Heavenly treasures store.

Eyes as clear as a sky of blue. For us Our Lady's love so true. Her blue gown is pristine. After her life's 7 sorrows; in heaven she's our Queen.

Printed in the United States
By Bookmasters